This book belongs to:

45377086R00068

Made in the USA
San Bernardino, CA
28 July 2019